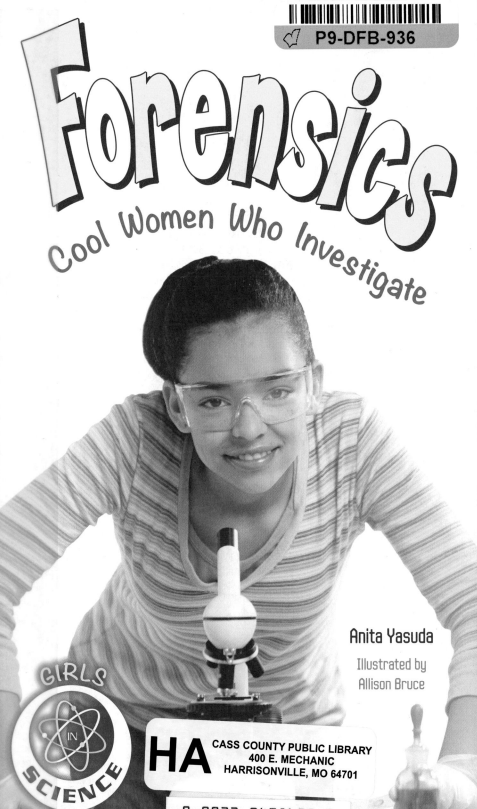

Forensics

Cool Women Who Investigate

Anita Yasuda

Illustrated by
Allison Bruce

GIRLS IN SCIENCE

Nomad Press
A division of Nomad Communications
10 9 8 7 6 5 4 3 2 1

This book was manufactured by Marquis Book Printing,
Montmagny Québec, Canada
March 2016, Job #121609
ISBN Softcover: 978-1-61930-350-8
ISBN Hardcover: 978-1-61930-346-1

Illustrations by Allison Bruce
Educational Consultant, Marla Conn

Questions regarding the ordering of this book should be addressed to
Nomad Press
2456 Christian St.
White River Junction, VT 05001
www.nomadpress.net

Printed in Canada.

~ Titles in the **Girls in Science** Series ~

How to Use This Book

In this book you'll find a few different ways to further explore the topic of women in forensics.

The essential questions in each Ask & Answer box encourage you to think further. You probably won't find the answers to these questions in the text, and sometimes there are no right or wrong answers! Instead, these questions are here to help you think more deeply about what you're reading and how the material connects to your own life.

There's a lot of new vocabulary in this book! Can you figure out a word's meaning from the paragraph? Look in the glossary in the back of the book to find the definitions of words you don't know.

Are you interested in what women have to say about forensics? You'll find quotes from women who are professionals in the forensics field. You can learn a lot by listening to people who have worked hard to succeed!

Primary sources come from people who were eyewitnesses to events. They might write about the event, take pictures, or record the event for radio or video. Why are primary sources important?

PS

Interested in primary sources? Look for this icon.

Use a QR code reader app on your tablet or other device to find online primary sources. You can find a list of URLs on the Resources page. If the QR code doesn't work, try searching the Internet with the Keyword Prompts to find other helpful sources.

CONTENTS

Forensics Labor

INTRODUCTION
What Is Forensics?

Under the sheets, with your light's battery running low, you can't stop yourself from turning to the next page. You're eager to solve this crime. The book clutched between your hands has everything that makes a great story. It has elements of suspense, multiple suspects, a sprinkling of clues, a red herring, and a great detective. Before the mystery is solved, there will be twists and turns. Then it will be brought to a satisfying conclusion with the criminal revealed.

In real life, solving crimes is much more challenging. It takes longer than the average novel or 52-minute television drama. The scene of the crime has to be secured, witnesses interviewed, and evidence collected—from carpet fibers to blood and hair.

Sometimes, the trail goes cold. The investigation might stall for months or years until new evidence is revealed. A hunch is not enough. That's why the people investigating crimes turn to forensic science.

Cool Careers: Forensic Botanist

Forensic botanists use their training in plant sciences to connect plant materials, pollen, microorganisms, and other evidence from crime scenes to suspects. British forensic botanist Patricia Wiltshire specializes in pollen and spores. She has been brought in to work on investigations with every police force in England, Wales, and Ireland and with four in Scotland. "An ecologist has to know a bit about everything," she says. "It's no good knowing just about plants, you've got to know about the soil they grow in. If you go to a crime scene, you've got to know what the creepy-crawlies mean. What are they feeding on, why are they there?"

Ask & Answer

What is forensics? Why should forensics be used to determine a person's guilt or innocence?

Forensics is when science is used to study and explain crimes in laboratories and in courtrooms. Forensics uses different branches of science, including biology, chemistry, medicine, and toxicology. In books or on TV, one person often appears to have training in all these areas. But this is not the case in real life.

Each area of forensic science requires specific study. A forensic botanist, for example, trains in biology, botany, or both! Some jobs are only available for police officers.

The American Academy of Forensic Sciences (AAFS) represents the wide variety of professions. The AAFS is the largest forensic organization in the world, with about 7,000 members. In 1948, the organization formed to promote forensic science education and improve the science.

An AAFS member might be a criminalist who analyzes data to understand why criminals commit crimes, or she might be an odontologist who examines the dental evidence.

In this book, the term "forensic science" describes the work of all these professionals. You'll learn about the history of forensics, including the tools and techniques used to identify suspects and solve crimes or other mysteries. You will read about different kinds of forensic investigators and learn about some detectives and scientists from the past and present. Plus, you will meet three women working in forensics today, and find out what inspired them to pursue their careers.

Christine Gabig-Prebyl is a forensic scientist with Douglas County Sheriff's Office in Nebraska and an instructor at Nebraska Wesleyan University. Jessica Frances Lam is a PhD student and researcher at England's University of Leicester Interdisciplinary Training and Research Programme for Innovative Doctorates (INTREPID) Forensics Programme. Stephanie Kristen Callian is a forensic scientist with the Orange County Crime Lab in California.

These women will share a typical day on the job with you. You'll get to read about how they use their forensic training to help law enforcement solve crimes. And you'll see how they teach new generations of forensic scientists and develop techniques and skills to study the evidence. You'll also learn about the challenges each woman faces and what they like best about their work. Maybe these women will inspire you to pursue a career in forensics, too.

CHAPTER 1

Fingerprints and the Future

Imagine finding that your home has been robbed. You quickly call the police, and investigators arrive to solve the case. They examine the scene and record their findings. The physical clues, including fibers and hair on your carpet and tire tracks in the driveway, will be analyzed back at the lab. Ideally, the criminals will be brought to a swift justice.

Not long ago, people investigating crime did not have the range of scientific tools or techniques we do today. Often, they did not even have records on criminals. Some people decided that there ought to be a more organized way to solve crimes and catch the people responsible.

The fingerprint was one of the earliest forensic tools used by investigators to find the right suspect. People have been using fingerprints for identification for thousands of years. People in Babylon, a city in modern-day Iraq, used fingerprints as seals on business contracts 4,000 years ago. In China during the Qin Dynasty (221 to 206 BCE), handprints were used as evidence. This remarkable fact is found in a document called *The Volume of Crime Scene Investigation—Burglary.*

In Europe, it wasn't until the nineteenth century that fingerprints were seen as a way to catch criminals. Beginning in 1858, Sir William James Herschel (1833–1917) began experimenting with prints.

66 I didn't invent forensic science and medicine. I just was one of the first people to recognize how interesting it is. 99

—Patricia Cornwell,
best-selling crime author

Sir William collected samples of fingerprints. After examining the samples, he realized that they could be used to identify a person.

Sometime later, an English police officer named Edward Henry (1850–1931) and his assistants began using fingerprints as a forensic tool. Edward developed his interest in prints after reading a book on fingerprinting by Sir Francis Galton (1822–1911).

In 1896, while stationed in India, Edward began working on a fingerprint classification system. He noticed that there are three main patterns of fingerprints—loops, arches, and whorls.

Sir Francis Galton

Sir Francis Galton was also interested in meteorology, geography, psychology, statistics, and genetics. You can learn more about him and even read his book on fingerprints. What do you notice about the language in his book? Does it sound different from books published today?

Francis Galton fingerprints

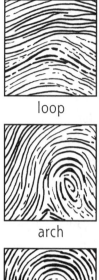
loop

arch

In 1900, he published the book *Classification and Uses of Fingerprints.* Throughout the nineteenth and twentieth centuries, the Henry System, which required a set of 10 fingerprints per individual, became the most successful way to identify and catch criminals around the world.

In the United States, the Federal Bureau of Investigation (FBI) began collecting fingerprint data in 1924. The database, which later came to be called the Integrated Automated Fingerprint Identification System (IAFIS), grew to be the largest criminal fingerprint database in the world.

whorl

Technology is always improving. The FBI replaced the IAFIS database in 2014 with Next Generation Identification (NGI). NGI stores biometrics information, which gives a lot more information than just fingerprints.

Ask & Answer

Can you think of any technology you use that has improved in your lifetime? Has it made your life better? How?

Biometrics are unique physical characteristics, including finger and palm prints, eyes, and facial features, that can be used to identify a person. NGI is the largest database of its kind in the world.

YOUR FINGERPRINT

Take a careful look at the tiny ridges on the tips of your fingers. These are your fingerprints. The chance that two unrelated people will have the same prints has been estimated as less than one in tens of billions. That's incredibly rare!

Your prints formed before you were born. Even if your fingers become damaged, the same pattern will try to grow back. Fingers leave prints because the ridges have tiny pores where oil and sweat collects.

Investigators look for three types of fingerprints. Patent prints are easily seen. They are made when a finger touches a substance such as blood or grease. A plastic print is made when a finger touches a soft surface like soap. A latent print is created by the pores on the finger. Often, the eye cannot see them until a dusting powder, laser, or other technique makes them visible.

> 66 Fingerprints can not lie, but liars can make fingerprints. 99
>
> **—rephrase of an old proverb in the** *Journal of Forensic Sciences*

SUPER SLEUTHS

It is not known when science first became part of law enforcement. An early example comes from thirteenth-century China. The book *Xi Yuan Ji Lu (Collected Cases of Injustice Rectified)* tells of a detective named Song Ci who was investigating a murder. The victim was killed with a sickle, which is a tool used to cut grain.

Song questioned the witnesses, but could not discover the culprit. So he demanded that the suspects bring their sickles before him. On the hot day, flies landed on the one with traces of blood and human tissue on it. The owner then confessed to the crime.

Dr. Gail Anderson

Forensic entomologists use their knowledge of insects to help solve crimes. By observing insects, they can estimate the time of death or tell if a body has been moved. Dr. Gail Anderson of Canada is one of only a handful of forensic entomologists in the world. She works on criminal cases, appears in court, and lectures at the School of Criminology at Simon Fraser University. She says, "We can use insects to work out where the wound sites were when they are no longer visible to the naked eye or to the pathologist." You can watch a video of her explaining her latest forensic project, which she keeps in a very strange place for bugs—the ocean!

Gail Anderson ocean forensics

A later example comes from France. In 1810, the Paris police department hired Eugene Francois Vidocq (1775–1857) to lead the first undercover police agency in the world. Eugene was a former criminal. He used his underworld experience to become a successful detective. His work resulted in more than 800 arrests.

Eugene also pioneered many new forensic techniques. He studied ballistics and made plaster casts of footprints. He recorded data on criminals, including their physical appearances and aliases.

FICTION AND FORENSICS

One detective who greatly influenced how crimes came to be investigated never even existed in real life! Sherlock Holmes used a combination of logic and science. Sherlock was a character in books by Sir Arthur Conan Doyle (1859–1930). Sir Arthur based the character on his former professor and forensic scientist, Dr. Joseph Bell. Sherlock Holmes first appeared in Sir Arthur's story, *A Study in Scarlet*, in 1887.

The public loved the Sherlock Holmes character. It was exciting to read about someone using science to solve crimes at a time when it wasn't common. Holmes turned his home into a crime lab with test tubes and Bunsen burners. Like a forensic scientist would today, he collected physical evidence, such as bloodstains and cigar ashes, and then tested them in his lab. He examined documents and fingerprints.

> 66 It's a capital mistake to theorize before one has data. Insensibly, one begins to twist facts to suit theories, instead of theories to suit facts. 99

—Sir Arthur Conan Doyle,
as Sherlock Holmes

Interest in Sherlock Holmes and his forensic genius inspired a real-life police detective. In 1910, Dr. Edmond Locard (1877–1966) set up one of the first official, dedicated forensics lab in the world. He secured a small attic space above a police station in Lyon, France.

At first, the police were skeptical, but Edmond showed them how science could be used to solve crimes when he helped break up a counterfeit coin ring. He used chemical tests to link traces of metal in the suspects' pockets to counterfeit coins.

Edmond is best known for one idea about physical clues. He believed that whenever objects or people came into contact, trace evidence was left behind. This idea is known as Locard's exchange principle. His methods were successful in solving hundreds of cases, earning him the nickname the "Sherlock Holmes of France."

Ask & Answer

Why do you think people were inspired by a fictional character? Do any fictional characters inspire you?

A New Sherlock

Sherlock Holmes is so popular that he still appears in hit movies, television shows, and books. Perhaps you have met his newly imagined sister, Enola Holmes, in the teen series of the same name by Nancy Springer? Like her older brother, Sherlock, Enola unravels mysteries by bringing her unique skills—including decoding ciphers—to the task.

CRIMINAL IDENTIFICATION

Before the police used photography and fingerprinting, it was not easy to keep track of criminals. There was no way of knowing if they gave their correct names.

In 1879, Alphonse Bertillon (1853–1914), who was working as a clerk in a Paris police station, created a system to identify criminals. The procedure came to be called Bertillonage. It identified people through 11 body measurements, including the length of the little finger and the width of the right ear.

Alphonse also standardized the practice of taking photos of criminals. These photos eventually came to be known as mug shots.

In 1883, after Alphonse Bertillon proved his system worked, the Paris police adopted his method. It became popular in Europe and North America. But there were problems with the system. Police found that people could share the same measurements. By the mid-1890s, Alphonse had to add fingerprints to his system.

In 1910, the French police asked Alphonse to find the thief who stole the *Mona Lisa* from the Louvre Museum in Paris. The thief had left a fingerprint behind. Unfortunately, Alphonse could not find a match for it. The print was from the thief's left hand, and Alphonse only kept records of right hands.

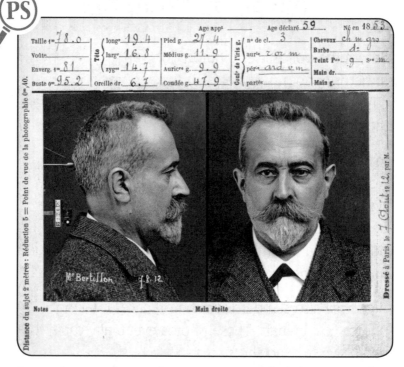

A sample mug shot and measurements of Alphonse Bertillon.

Ask & Answer

Why is it important to keep records of criminals? Do you think these records should be destroyed after the criminal has been released from jail? Do you think there are privacy issues at stake?

FORENSIC SPECIALISTS

Hans Gross (1847–1915) of Austria is considered to be one of the founders of forensics. He wrote a book called *Criminal Investigation* in 1893. It described techniques for bringing science into police investigations. Hans suggested that experts from fields such as chemistry, botany, and physics be used to aid in investigations. His book became a training manual for police.

Soon, police learned to deal better with blood evidence. In 1901, Karl Landsteiner (1868–1943) showed that human blood could be placed into groups according to how the blood collected together. Those groups are now known as A, B, AB, and O.

Another scientist, Leone Lattes (1887–1954), developed a test to determine the blood group from dried bloodstains. Blood typing can still be useful in criminal investigations.

"Nutshell Studies of Unexplained Death"

The first university program in legal medicine was established by Frances Glessner Lee (1878–1962) at Harvard in 1931. In the 1940s, Frances moved into police work and began working on crime scene dioramas. The 18 dioramas, titled "Nutshell Studies of Unexplained Death," allowed Frances to combine her interest in forensics and detective work. Frances, who came from a very wealthy Chicago family, often staged murder mystery dinners for guests.

But Frances didn't limit her world to high society. Instead, she talked to police officers and scientists to learn how they conducted and investigated criminal investigations. Her desire to create a tool that could aid in the study of evidence led her to create her miniature crime scenes. Frances's work is still used to teach forensic investigation. You can see pictures of her tiny crime scenes here.

Frances Glessner Nutshell Studies 🔍

A few decades later, scientists would make a discovery that would eventually be extremely useful to forensic science. In 1953, Rosalind Franklin (1920–1958) took a famous X-ray pattern image of deoxyribonucleic acid (DNA). This led James Watson (1928–) and Francis Crick (1916–2004) to discover the structure of DNA.

DNA is special because it contains the code for every cell in your body, from your hair and eye color to your height. This genetic information can be used to identify whether a sample at a crime scene came from a particular person. DNA is used in a way similar to fingerprints, only it's much more powerful.

DNA

A spiral chain of repeating parts called nucleotides.

Scientists use a process called DNA typing to produce a person's genetic profile. Researchers continue to develop new methods to identify people.

Facial recognition is another science that is rapidly improving. Computer software is used to compare a face to images stored on a computer. This software works by measuring 80 nodal points on a human face, such as the distance between the eyes.

Ask & Answer

Why is technology an important part of forensics science? Why are we always trying to improve technology?

Fingerprint Science

Sir Alec Jeffreys has been interested in science since he was a young boy. When he was eight, he even brought home a dead cat to dissect on the dining room table! This fascination served him well as he went on to discover DNA fingerprinting in 1984. Within a year, it was being used to solve forensic cases. You can watch a short interview with this scientist here.

Alec Jeffreys video interview 🔍

In 2015, researcher Linda Lewis developed a technique to help investigators rebuild fingerprints that have faded. What else is going to be invented? What other tools might be useful to forensic scientists?

JOBS IN CRIMINAL FORENSICS

Are you interested in science? Do you like to solve problems? Maybe there's a future career in forensics for you. It's an exciting and demanding field where scientific knowledge can be applied to many different jobs. Crime scene investigators have received special training in analyzing a crime scene. Photography, fingerprinting, and DNA collection are all part of this training.

When they arrive on the scene, investigators don't yet know what they will find or how important it will be to the case. They must carefully collect physical clues. These clues can be fibers, hair, blood, bone, and fingerprints. Mistakes are not allowed on this job, as evidence might need to be used in court.

Clues from the scene go to a forensic lab. Labs may be connected to a police force, the government, or owned by private companies. There are many questions these scientists must ask. They might need to know who the deceased was, and how and when they died. Using microscopes or chemicals, scientists conduct scientific tests on clues. When all the findings are put together, it is hoped that the mystery will be solved.

Another important job in criminal forensics is the role of the pathologist. Forensic pathologists are doctors who have done additional training. They need to know many different areas of forensics, such as the effects of weapons on people.

This is called wound ballistics. Forensic pathologists examine bodies to determine how and why they died. They might be asked to give evidence in court.

Ask & Answer

Why is it so important not to make mistakes in forensic labs? What happens if evidence in court is wrong?

66 It's very simple. When the barometric pressure dropped and the warm offshore air came in contact with an inland cold front we ran into some unnavigable nucleation. 99

—Velma,
teen sleuth from the TV show *Scooby Doo*

IF THE SHOE FITS

To acquire the skills needed in forensics, you will have to study at a university for at least four years. Some positions require you to be a police officer, while others need you to have a post-graduate degree. Most forensic scientists have at least a bachelor of science degree. Biology, biochemistry, mathematics, and forensic science are just a few of the courses included in a forensic program. Some schools offer specialist programs in forensic psychology or forensic anthropology.

Many young women are pursuing careers in forensics. According to the U.S. Department of Labor, forensic science is one of the fastest growing occupations for women. At Penn State University's undergraduate forensic science program, more than 70 percent of students are women.

In 2015, in Penn State's graduate program, 98 percent of students were women. Why this surge of interest?

Why is it important for women to have the same career opportunities as men?

Some people credit the high number of women enrolling in forensics to popular media. Television dramas such as *CSI* and *NCIS* feature female forensic scientists. The BBC's *History Cold Case* presents viewers with a real all-female forensic team. They use their skills to solve mysteries from the past.

There are novels, too, such as those written by Kenneth McIntosh and Alane Ferguson. Kenneth's *Crime Scene Club: Fact and Fiction* series showcases a group of young people using forensics to solve mysteries. Alane's mystery-thriller forensic series features Cameryn Mahoney, a 17-year-old aspiring forensic pathologist.

The Girl Scouts even have an "Uncovering the Evidence" badge with a silver fingerprint. It requires them to learn about forensic science by examining a crime scene, as well as learn other investigation skills.

Let's meet three dynamic women who work in forensics and find out what inspired them to pursue their careers.

CHAPTER 2
Christine Gabig-Prebyl

Ever since Christine Gabig-Prebyl was small, she loved reading mystery stories. Now, as a forensic scientist with the Douglas County Sheriff's Office in Omaha, Nebraska, she analyzes clues to solve cases of her own.

Christine was born on March 9, 1974. She is the oldest of three children. Christine's father, Joe Gabig, worked as a biologist, and her mother, Diane McDougal Gabig, stayed home and cared for the children.

When Christine turned four, her father was offered a job with the Nebraska Game and Parks Commission. So the family moved 1,000 miles west from State College, Pennsylvania, to Lincoln, Nebraska.

The prospect of moving fills some people with dread. For Christine, it was an opportunity to claim two places in the country as her home!

ADVENTURES CLOSE TO HOME

Christine had the heart of an explorer. Encouraged by her parents, Christine spent most of her time playing outdoors. Nebraska was the perfect playground for a curious person such as Christine. For the Gabig family, weekends were for exploring nearby forests, lakes, and rivers and wandering through seas of grassland.

Ask & Answer

Have you ever had to move? Was it a good experience? How did you handle the challenges?

These trips with her family enabled Christine to become a keen observer. There were always interesting objects to spy and animal bones to scoop up and examine.

She even collected owl pellets from an old barn for later inspection. By examining owl pellets, you can learn not only where the owl has been lunching, but also what it has been lunching on! Have you ever dissected an owl pellet?

Owl pellets contain evidence of the owl's recent meals.

What would you do if you found an injured critter along the trail? If you were Christine, you would bring it home in hopes of rescuing it. However, she soon learned that animal rescue wasn't easy or a particularly successful thing for the animal involved!

When Christine wasn't exploring nature, she was having adventures between the pages of books. An avid reader, Christine regularly rode her bike to the local library.

Nancy Drew

In the original *Nancy Drew* series, the heroine from the suburb of River Heights finds lost treasure and missing heirs, investigates sudden disappearances, and occasionally gets knocked out by crooks! Almost 85 years have passed since Nancy Drew debuted in the *Secret of the Old Clock*, helping the family of a dead man solve a mystery. Detective Nancy used intuition and forensics to solve crimes by deciphering clues from things such as footprints and clothing fibers.

The original series contained 56 titles. A new series called *Nancy Drew Girl Detective* came out in 2004. This series imagines Nancy as a professional detective using even more forensics to find culprits.

She looked for books with problems to solve, such as those in the classic *Nancy Drew* or *Hardy Boys* mystery series. *A Wrinkle in Time* by Madeleine L'Engle was another favorite.

To solve mysteries, you hunt for clues, spot patterns, and use the science that you know. For Christine, it was the crime-solving skills used in mystery stories that first attracted her to the science of forensics.

THE PATH TO COLLEGE

Christine's father was one of her earliest role models. He worked as a waterfowl biologist. It was through him that Christine developed a love for science. She enjoyed pouring over her father's old college textbooks and visiting him at his office. While he worked, Christine explored the Game and Parks Commission. She was fascinated with the rooms full of animal specimens and skeletons.

Her growing interest in science was further supported in high school. Her choices of classes were ones that discussed and questioned how things work.

The skeleton of a frog.

> 66 Students, especially those in forensic science, should read, read, read, and keep an open mind. 99

—Yolanda Thompson,
former director of the Trinidad
and Tobago Forensic Science Centre

Christine's classes included biology, chemistry, and physics. What is wonderful about science, says Christine, is that, "It can be applied to so many different fields."

Christine's parents believed that education was essential. They actively encouraged her to study. She tried hard in all her classes, and her work paid off when she graduated a semester early from high school.

Looking back on this time, Christine realizes that she should have taken some time to enjoy being in high school. Maybe she was too focused on what lay ahead. Now, as an adult, she tries to enjoy life more day by day.

When it was time for Christine to go to university, she knew what interested her. She enjoyed her science classes so much that she decided to major in biology at the University of Nebraska.

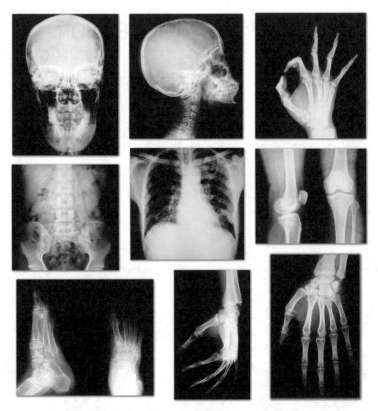

The different parts of the human body.

A biology degree requires classes in genetics and ecology. Christine, who was curious about the structure of the body, also took anatomy classes. At the University of Nebraska, the anatomy course uses models, images, X-rays, and real human cadavers. The emphasis on hands-on learning allowed Christine to gain a real understanding about how the human body works.

CHOOSING A PROFESSION

While earning her first degree, Christine only had vague plans for the future. When Christine graduated in December 1999 with a bachelor of science in biology, she wasn't sure what she was going to do. Initially, she had no plans for graduate school, but she wasn't sure what she saw herself doing for the rest of her life.

Emma Hergenreder

Emma Hergenreder graduated from the forensic science program at Penn State in 2015. She laughs about the *CSI* effect, but believes in it. "We would joke about it in our classes, but the '*CSI* effect' is a real thing in forensics. I fell in love with the field after watching shows like *NCIS* and *CSI*.

"I had always been more interested in science classes, so I was naturally drawn to the science behind the field. I took a forensics class that was offered at my high school and fell in love with the field even more. I was never bothered by the gruesome aspect of the job and I enjoyed the mysterious side to it. I never got tired of learning the material and I could never get enough of it. Even in my college classes, I enjoyed learning as much as I could. Forensics fascinated me.

"The major is nothing like the *CSI* shows, but I think that made me enjoy my work more.

Christine turned to her father for advice. He showed her an article that he had saved from the *Smithsonian Magazine*. Across the top of the page blazed the headline, "The lab sleuths who help solve crimes against wild animals." The article was about a wildlife forensic lab in Oregon called the Clark R. Bavin National Fish and Wildlife Forensics Laboratory. Christine was so intrigued that she phoned the lab. She wanted to know what sort of experience and education she would need in order work there.

"I liked the academically rigorous and scientifically based program at Penn State. I never had any experience in the field until after my junior year of college, when I interned with the Michigan State Police crime laboratory. There I saw the real-life side to my major and my love for the field grew even more. Going to work every day never felt like work. I was able to observe a lot of case work and even got to work on some case work myself.

"The most satisfying feeling I've felt to date has been watching a case go from start to finish, seeing a conviction come from hard work. I was always able to remove myself from the emotional aspect of the job — however, knowing that my effort helped make the world a safer place made the job that much more special. I still have yet to find a position, and I can't wait until the day I get to officially call myself a forensic scientist!"

MORE THAN AN INTEREST

Christine liked the idea of studying forensics and decided to return to school. She began searching for a program right away. She applied to three of the top forensic graduate programs in the United States—it was a competitive process. Around the same time, a show about a group of forensic investigators called *CSI* debuted on TV. Because of the popularity of the show, more people wanted to study forensics.

Christine was crushed when two of the schools rejected her applications. But a third letter kept her dream on track. The University of New Haven in Connecticut had a spot for her!

However, the offer was conditional. Christine had to prove that she could achieve good grades during her first half-year at school. As an undergraduate, she had excelled in some classes, but not in others. Christine says that her grades reflected her interests. Though her parents had warned her to keep an eye on her grade-point average, or GPA, she hadn't. She didn't think her grades would have an affect on her future plans because she hadn't even dreamed of them yet!

While the school's conditions did put pressure on her, Christine looked forward to the next big step in her life.

Ask & Answer

What has inspired you to pursue an interest? Do you see yourself holding that interest in the future?

After arriving in Connecticut, she had no time to feel homesick. It was a very exciting time for her in a new city, with a new apartment, school, and friends. And it was Christine's first opportunity to immerse herself in forensics.

During graduate school, Christine's classes had more female than male students. She sees this as a continuing trend in the forensic science classes that she teaches at Nebraska Wesleyan University. "Traditionally, the science fields have been dominated by men, so it is wonderful to be surrounded by so many brilliant young women," she says. "There is a lot of attention to detail and thinking outside of the box that is needed in forensic science. I think women tend to be very good at these things."

66 Nancy, every place you go, it seems as if mysteries just pile up one after another. 99

—Carolyn Keene,
author of the *Nancy Drew* series

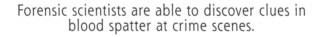

Forensic scientists are able to discover clues in blood spatter at crime scenes.

Courses in the University of New Haven's forensic science program includes crime scene reconstruction, analyzing bloodstain patterns, law and evidence, forensic anthropology, and toxicology. Christine found the program amazing! She liked taking courses from different experts and gaining hands-on experience through labs.

Christine took her classes seriously and excelled. When Christine graduated in 2003 with a master of science in forensic science, she felt ready for her career.

Ask & Answer ────────

Do you get better grades in the classes you enjoy? Why or why not?

Cool Careers:
Crime Scene Investigator

Crime scene investigators are usually some of the first people on the scene of the crime. They are responsible for securing the scene to prevent any contamination, collecting evidence, photographing the scene, and testing evidence for clues. They work at the crime scene and in the lab, but they never interact with suspects or other people involved in the crime. They work closely with law enforcement to ensure a speedy, truthful outcome.

WORKING IN FORENSICS

After graduate school, Christine worked as a crime scene investigator for many years. She looks back on this time and says that she was lucky to have the chance to work on so many interesting cases.

Being a crime scene investigator is very rewarding. But Christine points out that the job is tough. Investigators rarely work regular hours from 9 to 5. They can be called out to a job at any time of the day or night. This could be in the middle of the night, on weekends, and on holidays. Securing and analyzing a crime scene can't wait.

Ask & Answer

What are some benefits to having challenging tasks at work? Do you like work that is harder or easier to accomplish?

After Christine had a family, she decided it would be better to move into a position with more manageable hours. Today, she works as a scientist in the crime lab at the Douglas County Sheriff's Office in Omaha. No two days in the lab are ever exactly the same. Each case brings a new set of challenges, which Christine finds exciting.

Depending on the case they are assigned, lab scientists might need to spend hours or weeks analyzing samples. To get the job done, Christine combines science with problem-solving every day. This is why she refers to her position as "truly the perfect job" for her.

A DAY IN THE LIFE

What's an average day in a crime lab? The truth is that there isn't an average day. For Christine, she might be working on analyzing evidence from several different projects. There are proper procedures for her to follow. Evidence has to be handled carefully to avoid contamination.

All evidence is carefully documented to show a proper chain of custody. The chain of custody includes who collected the evidence, how it was packaged, when and where it was sorted, and when and to whom it was transferred.

In the different areas of the lab, Christine could be busy conducting drug or fire analysis. For charges involving illegal drugs, she has to test unknown substances before a person is charged.

Accuracy is crucial. As Christine points out, sometimes a suspected drug could turn out to be an innocent substance, such as sugar.

A reliable way to test samples is to use gas chromatography (GC) and mass spectrometry (MS). Gas chromatography separates the parts of a sample by heating the substance up until it becomes a gas. The gas travels along a metal tube. As it travels, the various chemicals within the gas separate and travel at different rates, based on their molecules.

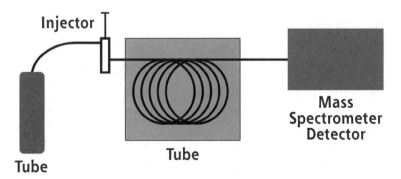

This diagram shows what happens inside a GC-MS instrument.
Credit: KMurray

A mass spectrometer will analyze the chemicals further to determine what they are. It does this by bombarding the chemicals with electrons that break them into fragments. The weight of each fragment creates a unique fingerprint or spectrum that a trained specialist such as Christine uses to identify the chemical.

Mass spectrometry is often used in investigations of arson. For cases that may involve a suspicious fire, Christine looks for ignitable liquids that may have been used to start a fire. Her results go to a fire investigator who determines whether or not a person should be charged with arson.

Christine also performs analysis on physical evidence, called trace evidence. She examines hair, fibers, and paint. Christine says that in her line of work, it is possible to find everything from glitter to rat poison! To identify and study this type of evidence, Christine works with microscopes, different light sources, and infrared (IR) spectrometers.

Each wave on the light spectrum has a specific wavelength. Christine uses different wavelengths to investigate different clues. Infrared is a region of the light spectrum that is invisible to our eyes. In the lab, Christine focuses the beam of light from an IR instrument on a sample to determine what it is. Her tests might reveal an important part of the crime story. They could link a suspect to a victim or a crime scene.

Lots of Uses for Infrared Light!

Infrared light is used in many different fields, not just in forensic science. Astronomers use infrared light to detect objects in the universe that we can't see because gases surround them or because they don't emit any visible light. Some doctors use infrared light to discover what's going on in a patient's body without having to perform exploratory surgery or use other painful techniques. Archaeologists and people who work to conserve artwork use infrared light to discover the chemical makeup of artifacts and art.

Christine also spends part of each day writing reports. Forensic scientists need excellent communication skills. Christine's reports inform courts of her findings.

She might also be asked to testify as an expert witness. Sitting in front of a judge and jury, she has to explain clearly which samples she analyzed and how she did it. She must explain her results, show how she arrived at her conclusions, and tell why they are important.

Christine once worked on a case that had more than 450 items of evidence from the crime scene! The case attracted a lot of media attention.

During the investigation, the police questioned a young man who confessed to the crime. He also said that his cousin was involved in the crime. The police arrested both men, but later, the young man took his story back. He claimed that he had confessed because of pressure from the police.

Christine went to work examining the evidence, which included a flashlight, ring, and shoeprint. She noticed that some clues did not point to those two suspects. Three pieces of evidence pointed to an unknown suspect or suspects.

Next, Christine turned her attention to an engraved ring that had been found at the crime scene. After much investigative work, Christine traced the ring back to its original owners. They had bought the ring in another state.

The case ended up involving four states. Finally, the police arrested the true culprits and released the innocent men. Christine says this case shows how important it is to examine each piece of evidence, as "it could turn out to be the key to solving a case!"

At the end of her long day, Christine faces a familiar challenge for busy people. She has to stop thinking about work when she comes home. When she is working on a particularly challenging case, she might think about all the possible solutions late into the night, when she should be sleeping!

Have you had problems that you were trying to solve that kept you awake at night? What are some ways you resolve your problems?

Christine says that one of the most awesome parts of her job is using science "to help find out the truth." Her findings could prove if someone is guilty or innocent. Christine feels that she is helping people with what she does each day.

TEACHING FORENSICS

Christine shares her first-hand knowledge of forensics at Nebraska Wesleyan University in Lincoln. She teaches several courses in the master's of forensic science program, including the fundamentals of crime scene investigation. Her seminars include topics such as DNA evidence and ballistics. For Christine, one of the best things about teaching is meeting students who share her passion for forensics.

As a teacher, Christine encourages her students to actively seek out knowledge, evaluate it, and form opinions. She likes them to ask questions and look for the solutions. She is also generous with her time and happy to demonstrate answers to students who are working hard as they pursue careers in forensics.

How Tiny? Pico Tiny!

Micro means tiny, and nano is even tinier, but there is a unit even smaller than that. It's a pico! The GC-MS that Christine uses in her work is an incredibly sensitive instrument. It can detect chemicals as small as a picogram. A picogram is 1 trillionth of a gram. A paperclip weighing one gram would be 1 trillion picograms!

The GC-MS is used to identify many substances, including chemicals in air, water, soil, plants, and animal tissue. In forensics, a scientist such as Christine might come across a sample that contains an unknown chemical. Mass spectrometry helps her to determine the unique chemical structure. The structure is like a fingerprint. Scientists take the result and compare it with the fingerprints of known chemicals.

When Christine was becoming a forensic scientist, her professors demanded a lot from her. She also expects her students to put in solid efforts.

In her role as a mentor, Christine helps students realize that mistakes are critical. Everyone makes mistakes she says, "and accepting that and learning a lesson from a mistake helps you grow as a person."

KEEPING UP WITH SCIENCE

It's important for forensic scientists to keep up with the new knowledge in their field. They need to educate themselves about the latest findings in a science that changes constantly.

Many forensic scientists attend yearly conferences. These are opportunities to talk to peers and listen to presentations that provide up-to-date information, from the newest legislation to the latest technological advances. Forensic scientists also take classes to strengthen their forensic training.

Several organizations offer courses, workshops, and certifications for forensic professionals. There is the International Society of Environmental Forensics (ISEF), the American Academy of Forensic Sciences (AAFS), and the American Board of Criminalists (ABC). Crime scene reconstruction and photography, advanced forensic techniques, and case studies are just a few examples of the classes offered.

Ask & Answer

When you have made a mistake, how have people responded to you? How were you able to learn from this mistake?

During her career, Christine has taken many such classes to keep her skills sharp. She has learned how to use a polarized light microscope to study human and animal hair, how to collect fire debris samples, and how to present information to a jury. Christine calls the opportunity to take classes "awesome." What makes them so great is that they are about something she enjoys doing!

ADVICE FOR FUTURE SCIENTISTS

"Working in forensics is amazing!" Christine says. She looks forward to work almost every day. She suggests that if you want to get into the field of forensics, you should consider taking as many science classes as you can in high school. "You can ask questions and explore new things," she says. "Science in real life is amazing!"

Christine also recommends finding a mentor. Someone at your local police station or crime lab might be willing to talk to you about their profession. A mentor may be able to suggest colleges or courses.

Ask & Answer

Why are mentors important? If you were a mentor to someone, what would you say to encourage them?

Fish and Wildlife Forensics

The Clark R. Bavin National Fish and Wildlife Forensics Laboratory officially opened in July 1989. It is the only lab of its kind in the world dedicated to solving crimes against wildlife. Scientists here examine, identify, and study evidence, just like investigators in a regular crime lab. Instead of evidence such as fingerprints, they examine parts of animals, from kangaroo hides and leopard skins to sea turtle heads and bear paws. The lab scientists try to piece together a jigsaw puzzle of physical clues that link their animal victim to a suspect or suspects. In 1998, the lab became the official crime lab of the Wildlife Working Group of Interpol, the world's largest network of police forces, and the Convention on International Trade in Endangered Species (CITES). You can learn more here.

Bavin Wildlife Forensic Laboratory 🔍

You can read the article that inspired Christine here.

FWS lab articles Smithsonian 🔍

Perhaps you will even be able to shadow a mentor at work for a day. This is a great opportunity to learn first-hand about the real job. "Remember," says Christine, "forensic scientists were once students just like you. They want to see you succeed!"

CHAPTER 3

Jessica Frances Lam

Jessica Lam has a passion for science, a curious mind, and a love of challenges. This combination launched her into real-life forensic research that has taken her around the world! Currently, she is a PhD student in the INTREPID Forensics Programme at the University of Leicester in England. Jessica is busy using 3-dimensional technology in forensic investigations.

On November 16, 1990, in Toronto, Ontario, Jessica became the first person in her family to be born in Canada. Her brother, Nathan, was born eight years later. Jessica's parents, Vincent and Regina, were natives of Hong Kong. Even though they were busy working professionals, they still spent lots of time with their kids.

Jessica grew up in Canada, in the multicultural city of Mississauga. It's the sixth-largest city in Canada. Mississauga is located west of Toronto. At an early age, Jessica developed an interest in detective work. She kept an investigation notebook and made her own fingerprinting kit.

As a budding CSI, Jessica tried fingerprinting her parents. Only her mother was willing—Jessica's father did not want to go to work with bright blue hands!

Besides making her first strides into the field of forensics, Jessica played the piano and practiced martial arts, including karate and kendo. She also read everything. Once, she even got in trouble for reading at school when she wasn't supposed to be reading!

66 But by far the most beautiful and characteristic of all superficial marks are the small furrows . . . that are disposed in a singularly complex yet regular order on the under surfaces of the hands and feet. 99

—Sir Francis Galton (1822–1911),
scientist, explorer, and anthropologist

Between playing and reading, Jessica developed a great imagination. She says, "The ability to think creatively is a wonderful tool in forensic science. It allows me to brainstorm and approach problems with sometimes unconventional but effective solutions."

WONDERING WHY

Jessica has always been a curious person. As a young child, she loved asking questions. She always wanted to know why things happened. Now, as a forensic scientist, asking "why" has become an important tool in her investigations. Jessica's father encouraged her curiosity and eagerness to learn by showing her anatomy and physiology books from his college days.

These books sparked Jessica's interest in human biology. She enjoyed learning about the body from head to toe and all the parts in between. She wanted to know how the muscles and bones in the body worked together. These parts are called the muscular system and the skeleton.

Ask & Answer

When faced with a difficult problem, what strategies do you use to solve the problem? What do you do if those don't work?

Bones in Your Body

Your body has more than 200 bones! These bones support your body and protect your organs, such as your heart and lungs. Without bones, you wouldn't be able to move. Located within many of the bones is bone marrow, where blood cells are produced. Red blood cells carry oxygen around your body and white blood cells protect your body against disease. Learn more about how your skeleton works here.

kids health bones video 🔍

Jessica's mother also influenced Jessica's career path. Her mother documented significant family events by keeping detailed notes and carefully arranged photo albums. Later, when Jessica entered college, she found organization and documentation easy. She thinks she learned this skill from her mother's earlier example of careful notation.

Details are important to forensic scientists because they have to accurately and meticulously process evidence. Later, their findings will be put into documents and given to investigators. If they mislabel something, the results of the investigation could be completely wrong.

66 It's brains. Not brawn. 99

—Krishna Patel,
fingerprint expert

EARLY DAYS

When she was still young, Jessica thought about becoming a lawyer. But a lawyer's job is to represent the client. A lawyer does not always represent the truth. Then, Jessica discovered forensics. She likes the fact that forensic scientists don't argue for one side. They focus on uncovering and examining the truth.

In high school, Jessica was attracted to the sciences, including biology, human anatomy, and kinesiology. Biology is the study of living things, anatomy is the study of the body's structure, and kinesiology is the study of how people move. She also enjoyed French and philosophy. Jessica credits her teachers for making these subjects so interesting that she still enjoys being in school!

Besides working hard at school, Jessica played the piano for the school choir and sang in musicals. She also stayed busy with martial arts and soccer. This schedule might seem overwhelming to many, but Jessica feels that learning to balance so many different interests has helped her manage tasks today.

When it came time to think about college, Jessica knew that she wanted to study forensics. Fortunately for her, the school with the oldest forensic program in Canada was close by, at the University of Toronto, Mississauga (UTM). At UTM, students in forensic studies can pursue a second science major, such as biology, psychology, or anthropology.

> 66 I used to tell people when I first came that we considered forensic science a boy's town, but now it's more like a girl's world. 99
>
> —**Sylvia Buffington-Lester,** forensic scientist

Jessica's application to the college was successful. But admission to the forensic program is based on a student's performance in required first-year courses. These include chemistry, mathematics, and an introduction to forensic science.

Sue Black

A forensic anthropologist and professor, Sue Black is the director of the Centre for Anatomy & Human Identification at the University of Dundee in Scotland. Growing up, Sue didn't think that she would go to university, but her grandmother and her science teacher encouraged her to attend. In 1987, she graduated from Aberdeen University with a PhD.

Today, people around the world know of her work. During Sue's career, she has investigated high-profile criminal cases in the United Kingdom. She led the British mission in identifying bodies of victims found in mass graves from the Bosnian War, which raged from 1992 to 1995.

In this class, students learn about crime scenes and other areas of forensics, such as entomology, dentistry, and anthropology. During her first year of college, Jessica took the required courses for the forensic program.

In addition to going to classes, Jessica became a member of the UTM Forensic Society. She became aware of this student organization when the vice president of the Forensic Society came to one of her lectures.

Sue and her team's work is also featured on the BBC documentary science program *History Cold Case.* In each episode, the team uses state-of-the-art forensic science techniques, facial reconstruction, and a variety of historical documents to tell the story of the person behind the skeleton.

Sue's work in the field of anthropology has been recognized with several awards, including the prestigious Royal Society Wolfson Research Merit Award in 2014. She says, "Being a woman hasn't made any difference whatsoever. If you can do the job and achieve the goals, then you're the same as everybody else."

You can listen to a radio interview with her here.

Sue Black
BBC radio

The Forensic Society became one of the most important parts of her college experience. Jessica not only volunteered for a murder mystery play hosted by the society, but she also ended up in charge of planning the event. The club became the key to getting to know people on campus.

Unfortunately, at the end of Jessica's first year, she became discouraged with forensic science. She learned that employment opportunities for graduates were limited because job growth had not kept pace with the popularity of forensic science careers.

Faced with an uncertain job market, Jessica decided not to enter the forensics program.

A NEW MAJOR

Jessica thought about medical school. Though she was not entirely sure, she switched to a double major in anthropology and health science biology. At the same time, Jessica was elected president of the Forensic Society.

66 Take coursework in molecular biology, genetics, biochemistry, and forensic statistics, and be sure that you're emotionally able to handle the graphic nature of a crime scene. 99

—Joanne Sgueglia,
forensic scientist

During her first year as president, Jessica learned about the enormous amount of work involved in running a club. She organized events such as the Get Arrested for Charity fundraiser for Child Find Canada, an organization dedicated to the safety of children. For a small donation, club members took fingerprints and mug shots of participants.

Jessica arranged general meetings that became opportunities for students and teaching staff to meet. She also coordinated a firearms training course so that interested students could work toward their firearms license. This type of license can help a person if they want to work on a police force.

Jessica was also busy throughout the year with outreach events. UTM often hosts field trips for middle grade or high school students interested in forensic science.

A CHANGE OF HEART

Through her work with the club, Jessica was in contact with the forensic science department and was constantly reminded of her decision to leave. Plus, she still had friends in the program. One day, Jessica heard two of her friends talking about a challenging forensic science project they were working on. Jessica felt that she was missing out. She found her current program to be boring. She wanted to be working on the same challenges as her friends.

For months, Jessica had been thinking about reapplying to the forensic program. Now, she realized, was the time to act.

Jessica asked what courses she would need to take to catch up. Luckily, the new director of the forensic science program, Dr. Tracy Rogers, and the forensic science program administrator, Teresa Cabral, supported her application. They allowed her to advance into higher subjects.

Ask & Answer

Should your friends influence the decisions you make about your life? Why or why not?

> 66 It wasn't so much the work itself [that was hard], but dealing with my own emotions that might present themselves, as well as the emotions of those being affected by the scene. 99
>
> **—Kelly Ayers,**
> forensic scientist

Jessica thrived in the program. She decided to focus her studies on forensic anthropology. Her forensic classes were quite small, only 15 to 30 students, and the majority of students were girls. Jessica worked hard and did well. She knew she had made the right choice by returning to forensics.

When she began studying forensic anthropology, it gave Jessica satisfaction to think that her work might bring closure to a family struggling with the loss of a missing person. Jessica says, "This is primarily what motivates me and gives me a passion for what I do in forensic anthropology."

Jessica credits her mother with giving her the reason that drives her passion for forensic anthropology. Her mother taught Jessica never to take anyone for granted. It's a simple message, says Jessica, but it's one that she has never forgotten.

Cool Careers:
Forensic Anthropologist

Anthropologists study how people lived in the past and present, throughout the world. Forensic anthropologists use the science of forensics to solve mysteries and learn about events in the past. Sometimes these scientists are called "bone detectives." They often work closely with scientists in other fields, including criminologists, odontologists, and pathologists.

Forensic anthropologists might examine skulls and bones to build a profile of an individual. This might include the biological sex, age, height, or ancestry. A person's bones can reveal if a disease or injury played a factor in their death.

Forensic anthropology began in the early nineteenth century as a distinct branch of science. This is when it was used to solve two high-profile murder cases. By the twentieth century, it was being used to identify the remains of soldiers. In 1973, the American Academy of Forensic Sciences formally recognized it as a special field of forensic science.

Today, you will find forensic anthropologists working for the police, the courts, and international organizations. They help identify the remains of soldiers, as well as of murder victims or disaster victims.

WORKING AND STUDYING ABROAD

While at college, Jessica had many wonderful opportunities to work in other countries. Although she was hesitant about the idea when she began college, a professor encouraged her to apply for work abroad. The selection process, says Jessica, was very difficult. She had to compete with candidates from around the world.

Knowing that her professor had faith in her, Jessica applied for a bioarchaeology project on the small Greek island of Astypalaia. She got the job!

Jessica spent six weeks on Astypalaia, which is located between Athens and Rhodes. Since 1999, archaeologists with the Astypalaia Project have been excavating human remains at two large cemeteries on the island. Most of the burials date from about 2,500 years ago. At that time, a child who died at birth was placed inside a pot through a hole cut in the side. More than 2,000 burial pots have been discovered on the island.

Ask & Answer

Do you like to travel? What can you learn about yourself when you travel to new places?

Astypalaia Burial Pots

It's very difficult to excavate and study the burial pots found in Astypalaia. Forensic anthropologists have to work in a tight space and be very careful that they don't disturb the bones. These bones are very delicate and they disintegrate easily. By studying the remains of those buried in Astypalaia, researchers can discover a lot of information about the people who lived there, including their diets, their growth and development, and their dentistry.

You can read about the excavations here. Why do you think the people of Astypalaia buried babies in the pots? Do you think this practice shows respect?

Astypalaia burial pot 🔍

Jessica helped in the excavation of children's bones from these pots. Each bone had to be carefully taken out and cleaned. Some very delicate bones were lifted with tissue paper to prevent them from disintegrating. They were identified, measured, and recorded on an individual sheet that was photographed.

Not only did Jessica find the experience amazing, but she also enjoyed traveling and working with people from different countries.

Jessica found another unique opportunity in college, taking part in forensic casework. In 2011, she became part of a team of forensic anthropology field technicians. Since then, she has worked on several cases with different police agencies across the province of Ontario, Canada. This work has involved going to the scene. Once there, the team searches for, locates, and excavates hidden or clandestine graves and scattered remains.

WORK EXPERIENCE

Though she had changed majors, Jessica still managed to graduate in 2012 with a forensic anthropology specialist degree and a minor in biology. She then took some time off from school between her undergraduate and her master's degree.

Ask & Answer

What important new skills have you acquired through volunteer or work experiences? What did you learn about yourself?

She continued to be involved with the forensic science program through her work as a teaching assistant for the forensic identification courses. The forensic department also created a special role for her as its public outreach administrator.

Teachers contacted Jessica to arrange field trips, lectures, and activities, from DNA extraction to mock crime scene examinations. Jessica liked the teaching aspect of her job and enjoyed meeting students who shared her passion for forensic science.

Jessica was also busy working in an osteological laboratory at the university. In one lab, she worked with the remains of a First Nations people called the Huron-Wendat. Most descendants of the Huron-Wendat now live near Quebec City.

Grand Chief Paul Tahourenché and other delegates of the Huron-Wendat visit the lieutenant governor of Quebec in 1880.
Photo credit: McCord Museum

Ask & Answer

Why is it important to return the remains of ancestors to their descendants, if possible? What might this mean for a culture?

The gravesites, some dating to the 1300s, were excavated between the 1950s and 1970s to make way for development. Jessica helped document and prepare the individuals to be returned to the Huron-Wendat Nation.

In another undergraduate teaching lab where she volunteered, her work was noticed by an anthropology PhD student. He asked her to be his assistant and help collect data in Lisbon, Portugal. Jessica didn't hesitate to say, "Yes!"

Jessica was learning to take advantage of unexpected opportunities. Soon she was flying across the Atlantic Ocean "with casts of hand and feet bones in a knapsack." These would help her identify and sort skeletons at the National Museum of Natural History and Science in Lisbon. The museum's Luis Lopes Collection has nearly 1,700 skeletons, with about 700 available for study.

Once again, Jessica found herself relishing life in a different country. It was fun to discover a new culture. Jessica says travel has allowed her to learn and gain a broader perspective of the world.

GRADUATE SCHOOL

In 2013, Jessica returned to UTM for a two-year master of science program in anthropology. Her project used 3-D external imaging to study bones.

A few months into the master's program, she learned about a new program in Britain called INTREPID Forensics. Dr. Lisa Smith, a graduate of UTM, headed the program. Lisa was encouraging applications to the PhD program at Leicester University.

INTREPID had a project that interested her, which combined engineering and pathology. Pathology is an area of medicine that studies the causes and effects of diseases. The project at Leicester University used a micro-CT scanner to find bomb fragments in soft tissues, such as muscles, nerves, or fat.

Jessica was genuinely interested in the project. At first, though, she was unsure how a degree in engineering would help her to become a forensic anthropologist.

66 Bones tell me the story of a person's life—
how old they were, what their gender
was, their ancestral background. 99

—Kathy Reichs,
forensic anthropologist and crime writer

Human Osteology

Forensic osteology is when the study of bones, which is called osteology, is applied to the field of forensics. Scientists work with skeletal material to determine what caused an individual's death. This can help researchers learn more about disease, health, or funerary customs of the culture they are studying.

Jessica worked in several different labs, including an undergraduate teaching lab at UTM. In an osteology lab used for teaching, students learn to identify features of skeletal anatomy. They also identify trauma or learn to tell the difference between human and non-human skeletal material.

Her supervisor convinced her that the program could help her achieve her goals. Jessica began the application process and was accepted!

At the same time, she set out to finish her two-year master's program in an impressive 12 months. Jessica did this while working as a university teaching assistant, taking on between two to six courses. This meant handling more than 100 students!

She also worked as the outreach administrator for the forensic science program and an osteology assistant at Toronto's Royal Ontario Museum. Meanwhile, she worked on four different UTM research projects.

One project took Jessica to Japan to work with a skeletal collection that was part of the Nagasaki University School of Medicine. Jessica and her assistant began collecting data using a new method to estimate the age of skeletons in an Asian population. Besides collecting data, Jessica found time to explore the region.

Marcella Farinelli Fierro

One of the leading pathologists in the United States is Marcella Farinelli Fierro. Marcella was the model for author Patricia Cornwell's medical examiner Kay Scarpetta in a series of best-selling novels. She was born in Buffalo, New York, in 1941. Wanting to help sick people, Marcella pursued medical studies at the State University of New York at Buffalo School of Medicine and Biomedical Sciences.

INTREPID

At present, Jessica is living in England while studying at the University of Leicester. She is enthusiastic about the program and the INTREPID group. Even though everyone is working in different fields, says Jessica, she still feels part of a team and appreciates her growing network of contacts.

Jessica is working on the project with a micro-CT scanner. It is the same instrument used to image King Richard III's skeleton. You can read more about this on the next page. The micro-CT creates a 3-D image of an object. It produces cross-sectional images, or slices of the body, like slices in a loaf of bread. The CT slices are stacked together to create the 3-D image. In a hospital, a patient is placed on a table inside the CT imaging system. The X-ray source and a detector rotate around the patient. In micro-CT, such as the one used by Jessica, the sample rotates instead.

Though there were few women in medicine at this time, she was determined to pursue her dream. She earned her medical degree in 1966 and went on to study forensic pathology at the Cleveland Clinic Educational Foundation and at Virginia Commonwealth University. Marcella worked as a pathologist for more than 30 years, including serving as the chief medical examiner of Virginia until she retired in 2008.

Finding King Richard III

King Richard III (1452–1485) was crowned king in 1483. He only ruled for two years. On August 22, 1485, he was killed in battle fighting Henry Tudor (Henry VII). His body was thought to be buried by a group of Franciscan friars, but over time, any record of his grave disappeared. In August 2012, the Richard III Society and Leicester City Council began looking for the lost grave of King Richard III. You can learn more about how scientists from the University of Leicester identified the remains of King Richard III here.

Watch a 3-D video of King Richard's skull here.

The death of King Richard III in 1485 is considered the end of the Middle Ages in England.

University Leicester King Richard 🔍

micro-CT scan king richard skull video 🔍

Producing a good-quality, 3-D image is an important part of Jessica's work. To create such an image, she has to understand how the 3-D image is made and what the computer program is capable of. "This is one challenging part of my research," says Jessica. In June 2015, she traveled to Germany to receive more training on how to use the program.

After graduating, Jessica hopes to work as a forensic anthropologist consultant for the police. She wants to continue teaching. She would like to become involved in various research projects with other scholars from different fields. "I absolutely love the potential for truly ground-breaking research when different perspectives are combined," says Jessica. She also sees herself working with 3-D technology and exploring its application in forensic science.

ADVICE FOR FUTURE FORENSIC SCIENTISTS

During her studies, Jessica has been lucky to have the full support of her family, fiancé, and the professors who encouraged her. She advises young people who want to be forensic scientists to "just go for it!" Learn to recognize an opportunity and grab hold of it. Prioritizing goals is the first step to achieving them. Ask yourself which goals you absolutely have to achieve. You can be more flexible with fewer goals.

As Jessica's academic and work experience shows, taking chances in life is important. She suggests that if you feel that you are not going in the right direction, you shouldn't be afraid to take your time to explore other options.

With regard to forensic science, Jessica advises that you find a topic that you are passionate about. For example, if you love insects, then investigate forensic entomology. If you like chemistry or physics, then study forensic toxicology or firearms analysis.

Jessica adds that, because there are not many jobs in forensic science, you must have a real passion for it. "This passion will drive you and motivate you even when the path to a career in forensics is long and hard." That passion can get you noticed by people who might be able to help you. Because forensics is a small field, this is crucial.

66 I think the popularity of shows like *CSI* and *Law & Order* have really given attention and a 'voice' to forensic science where it was pretty quiet before. That being said, the attention that its popularity brings can also be a negative for forensic science, which is why the population as a whole needs to be educated on what forensic science can and cannot accomplish. 99

—Kimberly Kobojek,
forensic scientist

Lastly, Jessica suggests that you do your research. The way forensic science is portrayed in the media is extremely unrealistic. Because of this, you won't see what's on a television drama out in the real world. Still, she says, the field of forensics offers something for almost everybody!

"My work with skeletal remains, 3-D technology, and forensic science appeals to me so much because I love finding new approaches to existing problems. I also like the fact that I can draw from different backgrounds to do so. I can see direct applications of my research on practical situations, which motivates me to continue my work. The bonus is that I am contributing to forensic science, a field for which I have a passion due to its impact on society."

Ask & Answer

What are your top three strengths? How do you use your strengths at school? Do you expect these strengths to carry over into the rest of your life? Do you think your strengths and weaknesses change as you grow?

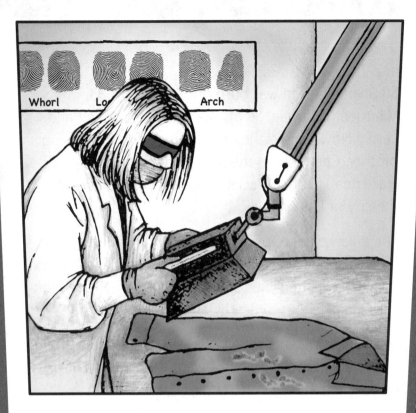

CHAPTER 4
Stephanie Kristen Callian

Stephanie Callian is a forensic scientist at the Orange County Crime Lab (OCCL) in southern California. The OCCL is one of the largest crime labs in the United States. It serves 100 different law enforcement agencies. For the past eight years, Stephanie has worked in the DNA section analyzing samples collected from crime scenes. This is quite a switch from her childhood passion of figure skating!

Stephanie Callian was born on March 2, 1983, in Whittier, California. Stephanie's parents, Joseph and Lesley Howl, raised their family, including her younger brother, Cameron, in the multicultural community of Hacienda Heights. Hacienda Heights is 19 miles from the city of Los Angeles.

The area was once primarily agricultural, but through the years it developed into a large residential community known for its tree-lined streets. Families commute from Hacienda Heights to nearby areas for work.

Stephanie's parents were both involved in sales. Stephanie, however, did not want to follow a similar career path.

Clea Koff

Forensic anthropologist and author Clea Koff is in the midst of an exciting career. She has worked for the United Nations, using her skills in forensics to investigate crimes in Rwanda, Bosnia, Croatia, and Kosovo. These are places where genocide has occurred, where many people have been killed and buried without record. She says, "It's a harsh reality to see when murder has become an acceptable political policy."

Clea has written a best-selling book based on her experiences called *The Bone Woman: Among the Dead in Rwanda, Bosnia, Croatia, and Kosovo.*

Part of it was that she didn't like the idea of doing the same thing every day. From an early age, she set out to find a field of work that she could feel truly passionate about.

  66 My interest in forensics really started when I discovered a nearly complete collection of Nancy Drew mysteries in my grandparents' basement. I was always getting in trouble for staying up too late reading under the covers **99**

—Renee Willmon,
biological anthropologist,
cold case investigator

She became interested in forensics as a college student in California. She was inspired by a book on a forensic team in Argentina that uncovered the remains of people who went missing during war in that country. After graduate school, Clea began her work with the United Nations. She and her team found evidence that was used to put war criminals behind bars. She currently writes mysteries.

To learn more about Clea Koff, watch this PBS interview.

Montgomery
Clea Koff video 🔍

Beginning in preschool, Stephanie attended the largest evangelical Lutheran school in the United States, St. Mark's Lutheran School in Hacienda Heights. Stephanie took school seriously and enjoyed the academic challenges at St. Mark's. After school, Stephanie could be found at the ice rink or reading. She was especially drawn to stories written by Lurlene McDaniel.

This American author is known for writing about teen characters struggling with illness and facing other life-changing events. Stephanie says the serious subject matter of these books first ignited her interest in life and death.

When her father lost his job, it wasn't possible for Stephanie to continue at St. Mark's. The family could no longer afford it. The move to a local public school midway through seventh grade was difficult. It was tough for her to leave behind the friends and teachers she had grown close to. The transition to a curriculum that Stephanie did not find as demanding was also hard.

Stephanie says that as a young girl, she felt that these were enormous challenges. In the end, though, these challenges served to drive her forward. Stephanie had an unflagging belief in education, and she told herself that if she wanted to get into a good college, she needed to study harder. She knew that a solid education would lead to a good job.

No one in her family had ever graduated from college, and Stephanie decided she would be that person. It would not only be her accomplishment, but her family's as well.

HIGH SCHOOL YEARS

Stephanie kept in touch with her friends and teachers from St. Mark's. When she learned from them of a high school fair being held at her old school, she decided to go.

At the fair, various high school representatives gathered to talk about what their schools could offer students. A challenging academic program called the International Baccalaureate (IB) at Sonora High School in La Habra caught Stephanie's attention.

The IB program is for students ages 16 to 19. It offers courses in six areas, including English, foreign language, and science. Though similar to Advance Placement (AP) classes, where students earn university-level course equivalents, IB classes require students to complete an independent research essay.

Ask & Answer

Have you ever had the opportunity to be the first in your family to do something good or amazing? How did it make you feel?

Ask & Answer

What can students learn by doing community service? Do you volunteer your time? Why?

The independent research essay enables IB students to demonstrate their writing and research skills. Students also participate in 150 hours of community service as part of the program.

Stephanie decided to apply for the IB program because it was more rigorous than regular high school courses. She worried about leaving friends again to attend school in an unfamiliar city, but she felt she would gain more opportunities.

She was accepted, and the IB program kept Stephanie busy. There were many late nights, but she soon learned how to balance academics and fun. Stephanie was a part of the Raiderettes, her school's dance and drill team. Almost every day after school, she practiced with her team, and Saturdays were often spent competing. By her senior year, she had become co-captain! After school, Stephanie volunteered as a children's skating instructor. She had begun figure skating at the age of six. These volunteer hours went toward her IB diploma.

AN INTEREST IN FORENSICS

Stephanie did well in school and especially liked the sciences. She enjoyed biology the most. "Bio classes tended to be toward the end of the day, too," says Stephanie. "So I felt like I always ended the day on a good note." The IB program coordinator, Robin Oliver, was one of the biology teachers. She became an important mentor to Stephanie.

During Stephanie's junior year, she felt pressured to begin thinking about what she wanted to do after high school. "On one hand," says Stephanie, "college was being described as a place where you would go to find yourself, to discover your true passions. But on the other, it felt like we were being forced to choose right then what our path would be."

It was at this time that Stephanie's math teacher sparked her first interest in forensics when he spoke about his brother, who worked as a forensic scientist. Also at this time, the popular television program *CSI: Crime Scene Investigation* aired.

66 Forensic scientists are not policemen. We are scientists. We deal with these matters objectively. We don't act on our suspicion. 99

—Cyril Wecht,
American forensic scientist

From her teacher, Stephanie learned how forensic scientists analyze evidence collected from crime scenes to answer questions such as who, what, where, and when. She also learned how forensic work could vary from day to day and how scientists could move to different positions within a lab. Stephanie was impressed. "This fluidity and freedom *really* appealed to me," she says.

Cool Career: Forensic Entomologist

Forensic entomologists use their knowledge of insects to assist in the investigation of crimes. They examine living and dead insects at a crime scene or on a victim. Some insects only live in particular areas and others are only active at certain times of the day. There are also insects that lay eggs on dead bodies. Based on this knowledge, scientists can determine where or when a crime took place or if a body has been moved from one location to another. Did you know that DNA can be found in the digestive tract of an insect that has fed on a person? Evidence such as this can be used to place suspects at a crime scene or even link a suspect to a victim!

Is it important to take both science classes and arts classes when you're young? Why or why not?

COLLEGE BOUND

When it came time to apply to college, Stephanie applied as a biology major. She reasoned that if she didn't like her studies, then she could always change her major later. As part of her program, she had the opportunity to take a humanities course, such as literature, art, music, and history. This opportunity, says Stephanie, "would satisfy my curiosity about what subject I really wanted to pursue."

Stephanie applied to four colleges and was accepted to Chapman University and the University of California, Irvine (UCI) as a biology major. Stephanie had only applied to Chapman because a friend of hers wanted to attend. Now she had a tough decision to make: go to Chapman with a friend or to UCI, which was known for its competitive biology program?

Stephanie decided that if she was serious about biology and pursuing a career in forensic science, then she had to choose a school that would benefit her in the future. That school was UCI.

Stephanie wasn't sure what to expect at college. Her teachers had spoken of the freedom she would enjoy deciding on her schedule. But, like many high school students, Stephanie found the transition from high school to college tough. UCI is a large school with more than 29,000 undergraduate and graduate students. Stephanie discovered that the school year was structured to run at an incredibly fast pace, with classes beginning and ending before she knew it.

66 You are just as capable as any guy in your class. If you love science, you can do it. Work hard and never forget *why* you like science. If you love your work, it won't feel like work at all. If you know it is what you want to do, no one else's opinion matters. 99

—Sarah Prebihalo,
PhD student in chemistry, University of Washington, Seattle

Dr. Jan C. Garavaglia

Dr. Jan C. Garavaglia's has a hit Discovery Health show called *Dr. G Medical Examiner,* which aired from 2004 to 2012. The program introduced people to the world of forensic pathology. Forensic pathologists investigate suspicious, violent, or sudden deaths. Then, they present their findings to the police, other pathologists, and lawyers. They even give testimony in court.

From a young age, Dr. G, as she is popularly known, was interested in science. Her interest in forensic pathology came as a student at the St. Louis University School of Medicine.

Also, UCI's biological science program was very competitive. Stephanie knew that she wanted to be in forensics, but she had to compete against students who planned to pursue studies in medicine or pharmacy. In fact, about 70 percent of UCI biological science majors say that they want to go on to graduate school.

Stephanie worked so diligently at college that she could have finished early. Instead, she added a minor in criminology, law, and society to her degree. She hoped that these courses would give her a better understanding of the law. Stephanie found the classes a great change of pace from biology.

Forensics allowed Dr. G to solve mysteries, and this aspect of the work appealed to her. After she finished medical school, Dr. G had the opportunity to study forensic pathology at the Dade County Medical Examiner's Office in Miami, Florida. In 2015, she retired as the chief medical examiner for Orange and Osceola counties. She had held the position since 2003.

One class that she took was "Forensic Science, Law, and Society" with Dr. Bill Thompson. The course looks at how forensic science, such as DNA testing or trace evidence, is used in criminal cases.

THE INTERN

After Stephanie had graduated from UCI, she began an internship with the OCCL. She had toured the lab while in her freshman year and from that experience realized it was the dream job for her. She didn't apply until her senior year because she felt that she couldn't take on an internship with her course load. To become an intern at the lab, candidates need two years of college chemistry. The lab staff conducts an interview and a background check before a person may begin working. They will even look at someone's history on social media, which is why it's important to only post things you wouldn't mind your future employer seeing.

Stephanie began work in the trace evidence section of the crime lab. This is where small pieces of evidence, such as samples of pollen, soil, fibers, or hair, are handled.

A gas chromatography-mass spectrometry (GC-MS) instrument is used to separate and identify components of each sample. Each profile is added to a library. Stephanie liked how much independence she was given, and "not necessary the freedom to try new things and discover how it turned out, even if it was wrong."

BECOMING A FORENSIC SCIENTIST

After Stephanie completed her internship, she applied to be a forensic scientist at the lab. The application process included a written exam, which she did not pass. While Stephanie was working on it, she realized it was not going well, but she did not give up. When it was over, she headed out to her car. Determined to do better the next time, she sat and wrote down all the questions that she could remember. When she got home, Stephanie researched the answers.

She had to wait an entire year before the position became available again. When it did, Stephanie applied and, this time, she passed the exam! The next step of the interview process required her to appear before a panel of three forensic scientists. Stephanie was crushed to learn that she didn't make it to the next round.

A few weeks later, she received good news: The lab wanted her to consider a job as a forensic technician. Stephanie accepted the position knowing that it was the perfect starting point to move up within the lab.

Stephanie Kristen Callian **85**

Ask & Answer

What do you do when you fail at something? Do you quit or keep trying?

She says that though the interview process didn't turn out exactly as she wanted, it was for the best. "Even though it wasn't what I wanted, it ended up being the best thing that could have happened to me."

In her position as a technician, she learned about how the entire lab functioned and how to resolve problems. It was a valuable experience she was lucky to have.

THE FORENSIC SCIENTIST

Stephanie now works as a forensic scientist in the DNA section of the OCCL. The crime lab has five sections, called bureaus. They deal with everything from identifying fingerprints, drugs, and toxic chemicals to comparing physical evidence, such as firearms and trace evidence.

The DNA section processes about 15,000 samples a year. These come from different types of cases, including theft, assault, and other crimes. DNA can be pulled from all sorts of evidence, from bottles to pillowcases. The OCCL uses robots to increase the number of samples that it can process.

Cold Cases and Innocent Prisoners

Using robots in forensics labs means that scientists can process their cases more quickly. It also means that old cases can be checked. People who were wrongly convicted of a crime many years ago might be proven innocent. Cases that were never solved, called cold cases, can benefit from DNA testing technology that wasn't available when the crime first happened. The Innocence Project is a group dedicated to helping prisoners who might benefit from DNA testing. Since the group was established in 1992, more than 300 people in the United States have been set free because of forensic DNA analysis.

It used to take scientists about four hours to process 24 DNA samples. Thanks to robotics, Stephanie says, "we can now process 80 samples in roughly the same amount of time."

A TYPICAL WORK DAY

Stephanie's official title is forensic scientist III, the most senior forensic scientist that conducts casework. To do this, she needs to have a solid understanding of all areas of the lab. Her knowledge was tested with a written exam and an oral panel interview.

After receiving a work request from the police, Stephanie figures out what has to be examined, such as blood or saliva. She must also decide the order in which the samples need to be analyzed. What goes first and what can wait until later?

Have you seen the *CSI* shows on television? On those shows, examining evidence sometimes takes less than an hour, but the reality is much different.

An average day for Stephanie begins at 6:30 a.m. for her nine-hour shift. Working this longer shift enables her to take every other Friday off from work. Each day in the lab is different. Stephanie might have to go through data from the previous evening and then make conclusions based on the results, or she may examine evidence. She says, "Evidence can be anything from a swab, which is basically a Q-tip on a really long stick, to clothing, to weapons, to beverage containers."

Prepared samples of bone are placed in a centrifuge, which spins the samples so fast that the DNA separates from the bone material.

Rapid DNA Technology

DNA technology was first used to help solve a criminal case in 1986. This is when Professor Alec Jeffreys, the inventor of DNA fingerprinting, was asked to aid in a criminal investigation. His findings helped solve the crime. Since then, there have been many advances in the way DNA is collected and processed. An exciting new technology called Rapid has the potential to change the length of time it takes to solve a crime. Rapid DNA technology can return a DNA profile in less than two hours instead of weeks. Right now, the technology is used in only a few states, but many labs are testing these portable machines that are about the size of a small photocopier. In the future, crime investigators might be able to bring one of these machines directly to a crime scene.

Stephanie only needs a small amount of DNA, less than 1 nanogram, to build a DNA profile. This is similar to a fingerprint. Once she has a sample, Stephanie breaks the cells open to release the DNA. This process is called lysis.

A series of steps allows her to measure how much human DNA is in the sample. Then, she uses a technique known as the polymerase chain reaction to make millions of copies of the DNA sample. Sometimes, Stephanie is called into court to testify about her results.

ENJOYING THE JOB

One of the coolest things about Stephanie's job is testifying in court. She likes explaining to a jury how she arrived at her results. Members of the jury might have little, if any, scientific training. She has to make sure that they understand what she is saying. "I look at testimony as a chance to educate," she says.

Although attending court as an expert witness is interesting, answering questions and solving problems are what Stephanie likes best about her job. Mostly, she answers questions for lawyers, but sometimes, "I even answer questions to police or law enforcement." She never speaks with the victim of a crime, which Stephanie says is a common misconception about her job, thanks to television.

66 . . . we don't have involvement with the family, for a very good reason—you can't afford to be influenced by their emotion and their situation. So the majority of our work is in clinical isolation. And you go the full 110 percent on everything you do, whether it's for the police, the courts, the family, whoever it is, it doesn't matter. 99

—Dr. Sue Black,
forensic scientist

Of course, all jobs have challenges. One challenge for Stephanie is that juries familiar with crime dramas have expectations for forensics that don't exist in real life. Juries might be familiar with DNA evidence, for example, but that isn't available in all cases.

Stephanie explains that just because a suspect's DNA was not discovered at a crime scene doesn't mean that the person was not there. It could simply mean that DNA couldn't be detected. Also, just because a person's DNA is at the crime scene, this doesn't mean the person is guilty!

CAREER ADVICE

Stephanie suggests that to become a successful DNA analyst, you might begin by investigating colleges with solid science programs. Chemistry and biology are examples of two possible fields of study. A forensic scientist needs an undergraduate science degree because they are required to apply scientific knowledge to criminal cases.

Ask & Answer

Do you ever get nervous when speaking in public? What helps you to stay calm and focused?

While a master's degree is not necessary, Stephanie says, "a lot of people have them, usually in forensic science, but you could also get a science graduate degree." A person enrolled in a master of forensic science program can specialize in different fields of forensics, such as forensic chemistry or forensic toxicology.

Forensics Lab Titles

Within a forensics lab, titles are used to reflect a forensic scientist's level of training and experience. At the OCCL, forensic scientist I is an entry-level position. This person is still learning how to process an investigation. They will assist more experienced personnel to learn about the different techniques used to handle or examine evidence and how to use specific equipment.

A forensic scientist II is an experienced scientist who can work more independently in the lab than an FSI. This person conducts lab analysis of physical evidence and might be asked to appear in court as an expert witness. Scientists in this class are still not expected to work entirely on their own. A forensic scientist III performs work independently within a lab and has knowledge of all the various sections.

Above this level is a forensic scientist supervisor, who oversees the entire lab. A supervisor's work includes planning and reviewing casework.

Learning never ends for scientists. To stay up to date on current research and developments, scientists such as Stephanie attend seminars and study sessions.

Stephanie is a member of the California Association of Criminalists (CAC) and the American Academy of Forensic Sciences. The CAC offers seminars for its members twice a year. Some crime labs require that scientists hold certain professional certifications for which they have to take tests to demonstrate their skills in a particular area of forensics.

It is also important, says Stephanie, for future forensic scientists to stay out of trouble. Almost all labs will do background investigations on new employees. If you have a criminal record or have otherwise gotten into trouble, you will not be able to find a job.

Stephanie suggests that get your foot in the door by taking a tour, applying for an internship, or accepting a lower position. She says, "If it's something that you really want, make it happen. It takes a lot of hard work and determination, but it is all worth it in the end. Coming to work every day doesn't really feel like work because I enjoy what I do so much."

Stephanie Kristen Callian 93

Timeline

500 BCE

- Fingerprints are used in the ancient city of Babylon to sign clay business contracts.

221 BCE-220 CE

- The Chinese use fingerprints for identification.

1248

- Chinese author and investigator Song Ci publishes what may be the first book on forensics called *Xi Yuan Ji Lu* (*Collected Cases of Injustice Rectified*).

1784

- John Toms is convicted of murder after newsprint found in his pocket is linked to the murder weapon. This is an early example of forensic clues being used for a conviction.

1879

- French researcher Alphonse Bertillon develops the first system of identifying criminals based on body measurements.

1843

- Belgium police begin keeping a type of photo called a daguerreotype to identify known criminals.

1887

- British doctor and author Arthur Conan Doyle publishes his first novel featuring Sherlock Holmes.

1889

- French medical researcher Alexandre Lacassagne publishes a paper explaining how a bullet can be traced to the gun it was fired from.

1892

- British scientist Sir Francis Galton publishes *Finger Prints*, which explains how fingerprints can be used to identify a person.

1893

- Austrian professor and criminalist Hans Gross writes a handbook for crime investigators called *Criminal Investigation: A Practical Handbook for Magistrates, Police Officers, and Lawyers.*

1895

- German physicist Wilhelm Conrad Rontgen discovers X-rays, which become an important tool in forensics.

1896

- British fingerprint expert Sir Edward Richard Henry and his assistants create a system to classify fingerprints.

Timeline

1898

- German chemist Paul Jeserich successfully matches a bullet from a crime scene to a suspect's gun.

1900

- British fingerprint expert Sir Edward Richard Henry publishes *Classification and Uses of Fingerprints*, which becomes the standard system of classification in Europe and North America.

1901

- Austrian biologist and doctor Karl Landsteiner discovers that blood cells fall into different groups that are later labeled as types A, B, AB, and O.

1910

- In Lyon, France, French criminalist Edmond Locard opens the world's first modern forensic lab.

1914

- The first forensic lab in North America opens.

1915

- Italian scientist Leone Lattes develops a method for identifying blood types from dried blood.

1920

- French criminalist Edmond Locard states his exchange theory, which is expressed as, "every contact leaves a trace."

1923

- The Los Angeles Police Department establishes the first crime lab in the United States.

1932

- The U.S. Bureau of Investigations (later known as the Federal Bureau of Investigations) establishes a lab that will become the center for forensics in the United States.

1940s

- American Frances Glessner Lee begins to build miniature crime scene models to train detectives.

1948

- The American Academy of Forensic Sciences is established.

1953

- British scientists James Watson and Francis Crick discover the structure of DNA after looking at an X-ray pattern image by Rosalind Franklin.

1960s

- Woodrow W. Bledsoe creates the first semi-automatic face recognition system.

Timeline

1965

- The first commercial scanning electron microscope (SEM) is produced, allowing detailed 3-dimensional images of samples to be created.

1970

- American professor Roland Menzel discovers lasers can locate fingerprints not visible to the naked eye.

1971

- British-born Canadian psychologist Jacques Penry invents the Penry Facial Identification Technique, or PhotoFIT, that uses photographs of features to identify suspects.

1984

- British scientist Dr. Alec Jeffreys discovers the first DNA "fingerprinting" technique.

1994

- British-American scientist John Daugman patents an iris recognition system.

1995

- Britain sets up the world's first DNA database containing DNA records of convicted criminals.

1998

- The FBI launches the National DNA Index System (NDIS) and the Combined DNA Index System (CODIS) software, a DNA criminal database.

1999

- The FBI introduces the Integrated Automated Fingerprint Identification System (IAFIS) which stores fingerprints and histories of criminals.

- The U.S. Bureau of Alcohol, Tobacco, Firearms and Explosives establishes the National Integrated Ballistic Information Network (NIBIN), containing images of ballistics evidence.

2004

- Connecticut, Rhode Island, and California launch the first automated palm print databases of known criminals.

2011

- Researchers in Michigan create software to match hand-drawn facial sketches to mug shots.

2014

- The FBI's Next Generation Identification biometrics database becomes fully operational.

Ask & Answer

Introduction

- What is forensics? Why should forensics be used to determine a person's guilt or innocence?

Chapter 1

- Can you think of any technology you use that has improved in your lifetime? Has it made your life better? How?

- Why do you think people were inspired by a fictional character? Do any fictional characters inspire you?

- Why is it important to keep records of criminals? Do you think these records should be destroyed after the criminal has been released from jail? Do you think there are privacy issues at stake?

- Why is technology an important part of forensics science? Why are we always trying to improve technology?

- Why is it so important not to make mistakes in forensic labs? What happens if evidence in court is wrong?

- Why is it important for women to have the same career opportunities as men?

Chapter 2

- Have you ever had to move? Was it a good experience? How did you handle the challenges?

- What has inspired you to pursue an interest? Do you see yourself holding that interest in the future?

- Do you get better grades in the classes you enjoy? Why or why not?

- What are some benefits to having challenging tasks at work? Do you like work that is harder or easier to accomplish?

- Have you had problems that you were trying to solve that kept you awake at night? What are some ways you resolve your problems?

- When you have made a mistake, how have people responded to you? How were you able to learn from this mistake?

- Why are mentors important? If you were a mentor to someone, what would you say to encourage them?

Ask & Answer

Chapter 3

- When faced with a difficult problem, what strategies do you use to solve the problem? What do you do if those don't work?

- Would you stop pursuing a degree in a field with few jobs? Why or why not? What are some ways you might achieve your goal?

- Should your friends influence the decisions you make about your life? Why or why not?

- Do you like to travel? What can you learn about yourself when you travel to new places?

- What important new skills have you acquired through volunteer or work experiences? What did you learn about yourself?

- Why is it important to return the remains of ancestors to their descendants, if possible? What might this mean for a culture?

- Do you feel it is better to spend more time on fewer activities or less time on more activities? Why?

- What are your top three strengths? How do you use your strengths at school?

Chapter 4

- Have you ever had the opportunity to be the first in your family to do something good or amazing? How did it make you feel?

- What can students learn by doing community service? Do you volunteer your time? Why?

- Is it important to take both science classes and arts classes when you're young? Why or why not?

- What is your reaction when you discover you were wrong about something?

- What do you do when you fail at something? Do you quit or keep trying?

- Do you ever get nervous when speaking in public? What helps you to stay calm and focused?

- Have you ever watched a crime show or movie about forensics? Do you think differently about forensics after reading about Stephanie?

98 **Forensics**

acid: a type of chemical substance with particular properties.

agricultural: growing crops and raising animals for food.

alias: another name someone is known by.

analysis: a careful study.

analyze: breaking down problems into small parts to find solutions.

anatomy: the study of the physical structure of living things.

anthropology: the study of human beings.

arch: a fingerprint pattern that looks like a hill.

archaeologist: a scientist who studies ancient people through the objects they left behind.

arson: to purposefully and illegally set a fire.

artifact: man-made evidence from a recent crime scene, or any man-made object that archaeologists study to learn about an ancient civilization.

avid: eager and enthusiastic.

ballistics: the study of the movement of objects that are shot through the air.

BCE: put after a date, BCE stands for Before Common Era and counts down to zero. CE stands for Common Era and counts up from zero. These nonreligious terms correspond to BC and AD. This book was printed in 2016 CE.

Bertillonage system: a system created by Alphonse Bertillon to identify criminals based on body measurements.

biochemistry: the study of the chemistry plant and animal life.

biology: the study of life and of living organisms.

biometrics: the study of physical or behavioral characteristics as a way to identify people.

blueprint: a model or template to follow.

botanist: a scientist who studies plant life.

botany: the study of plants.

brainstorm: to think creatively and without judgment, often in a group of people.

bureau: a group of people who specialize in a certain job.

cadaver: a dead body.

carrion: the dead and rotting body of an animal.

cast: a model of a shape, such as a footprint, made by pouring liquid form into a mold and letting it harden.

cell: the basic building block of all living organisms.

centrifuge: a machine that spins mixtures around at high speed. The spinning separates the mixture into its parts.

chain of custody: the order in which evidence from a crime scene is handled by investigators and documented.

characteristic: a feature of a person, place, or thing, such as blue eyes or curly hair.

chemical: a substance that has certain features that can react with other substances.

chemistry: the science of how substances interact, combine, and change.

chromatography: a method of separating the components of a mixture by differences in their attraction to a liquid or gas or solid.

cipher: a hidden message.

clandestine: secret.

classification: a way of organizing things in groups.

conditional: dependent on something, such as good grades.

Glossary

confess: to admit to doing a crime.

contamination: the presence of foreign material in a sample of evidence.

counterfeit: a fake version.

crime: an action that is against the law, or a failure to act that is required by law.

criminal: a person who has committed a crime.

criminalist: someone who specializes in studying crime.

criminologist: someone who specializes in studying crime.

criminology: the study of crime.

cross-sectional image: a picture that looks like it has been made into slices, as with a loaf of bread.

culprit: someone accused of a crime.

custody: when a suspect or evidence is held by the police in an investigation.

data: information in the form of facts and numbers.

database: a collection of data that can be easily searched.

debris: the scattered pieces of something that has been broken or destroyed.

deceased: dead.

decipher: to figure out the meaning of something.

decode: to decipher something.

deoxyribonucleic acid (DNA): the substance that carries your genetic information, the "blueprint" of who you are.

detective: someone who solves mysteries.

diorama: a miniature version of a scene.

disintegrate: to break down or decay.

DNA extraction: the process of taking DNA from a biological sample.

documentation: a written record of something.

dominate: to strongly influence.

ecologist: a scientist who studies the interaction between organisms and their environment.

electron: a part of an atom that has a negative charge. It can move from one atom to another.

emphasis: special importance.

entomology: the study of insects.

evidence: facts or arguments that prove a case.

excavates: to dig out material from the ground.

exchange principle: the theory that every contact leaves trace evidence behind.

facial features: the characteristics of your face, such as the shape of the nose, mouth, and eyes.

fibers: the smaller pieces or threads of a material that has been broken down.

fingerprint: the unique pattern of ridges on a fingertip.

firearm: a gun.

fluidity: the state of being fluid, or changeable.

forensic: the science of finding and analyzing crime scene evidence.

forensic archeologist: a scientist who recovers evidence and human remains.

fragments: a tiny broken piece of something.

funerary: associated with burial.

gas chromatography: a way of separating a substance into its basic parts.

genetic: related to the origin of something; things about you that are passed from parent to child.

red herring: a diversion, a false clue.

ignitable: able to be set fire to.

immerse: to become absorbed by something.

Glossary

infrared (IR): a type of light with a longer wavelength than visible light, which can also be felt as heat.

intuition: quick insight or knowledge.

investigation: a detailed investigation.

kinesiology: the study of human movement.

laser: a device that emits a focused beam of light.

latent print: an invisible print made from oils, perspiration, and other skin substances.

law enforcement: the police, prosecutors, and the judicial system.

legislation: the act of making new laws.

logic: the principle, based on math, that things should work together in an orderly way.

lysis: the process of breaking cells open to release the DNA.

mass: the amount of material that an object contains.

mentor: a person who advises and guides a younger person.

meteorology: the study of weather and climate.

meticulously: very precise and taking extreme care with small details.

micro-CT scanner: a machine that produces 3-D, X-ray images of specimens and artifacts.

microorganisms: a living thing that is so tiny it can only be seen using a microscope. Bacteria, fungi, and algae are all microorganisms.

microscope: an instrument that uses light to magnify the view.

molecules: a group of atoms bound together to form matter.

motivate: to give someone reason to do something.

mug shot: an identifying photograph taken when someone is arrested.

multicultural: made of different cultures and backgrounds.

nano: very small.

odontologist: a scientist who studies teeth and jaw bones.

osteology: the study of bones.

patent: having the exclusive right to make, use, or sell something.

patent print: a fingerprint made when a finger touches a substance such as blood or grease.

pathologist: a scientist who studies disease.

perpetrator: someone who commits a crime.

PhD: an education degree that shows mastery of a subject.

physics: the science of how matter and energy work together.

physiology: the study of the internal workings of living things.

pico: a very tiny unit of measurement.

pioneered: to be the first to do or discover something.

plaster: a sculpting material that hardens into the shape of the container it's poured into.

polarized light microscope: a microscope that uses polarized light, or light with a single wavelength.

pollen: a fine, yellow powder produced by flowering plants. Pollen fertilizes the seeds of other plants as it gets spread around by the wind, birds, and insects.

pores: a tiny opening through which substances pass.

principle: an important idea or belief that guides an individual or community.

psychology: the science of the mind and behavior.

reconstruction: the act of rebuilding something.

represent: to stand for something.

crime scene: the location of a crime.

secure: to make safe.

sickle: a sharp farming tool in the shape of a half moon.

Glossary

specimen: a sample of something.

spectrometer: a device used to identify chemical composition by analyzing light waves.

spectrum: a range of things with similar qualities.

spores: a structure produced by fungi that sprouts and grows into a new fungus.

statistics: numbers that show facts about a subject.

suspect: a person who might be guilty.

suspense: a feeling or state of nervousness or excitement caused by wondering what will happen.

theories: an idea or set of ideas intended to explain something.

theorize: to come up with an idea that explains how or why something happens.

tissue: a large number of cells similar in form and function that are grouped together.

toxicology: the study of poisons.

trace: a very small amount.

unconventional: not traditional.

undergraduate: the first level of college education.

wavelength: the distance from crest to crest in a series of waves.

whorl: a ridge pattern that forms a spiral that looks like a complete circle.

witness: someone who sees a crime happen.

wound: an injury.

Resources

Books

- Bragg, Georgia. *How They Croaked: The Awful Ends of the Awfully Famous.* Bloomsbury USA Childrens, 2012.
- Cooper, Chris. Forensic Science: *DK Eyewitness Book.* DK Children, 2008.
- Gardner, Robert. *Whose Bones Are These?: Crime-Solving Science Projects.* Enslow Elementary, 2010.
- Jackson, Donna M. *The Bone Detectives: How Forensic Anthropologists Solve Crimes and Uncover Mysteries of the Dead.* Little, Brown Books for Young Readers, 1996.
- Mooney, Carla. *Forensics.* Nomad Press, 2013.
- Mooney, Carla. *Genetics.* Nomad Press, 2014.
- Murray, Elizabeth A. *Forensic Identification: Putting a Name and Face on Death.* 21st Century Books, 2012.
- Murray, Elizabeth A. *Death: Corpses, Cadavers, and Other Grave Matters.* 21st Century Books, 2010.
- Schulz, Karen. *CSI Expert! Forensic Science for Kids.* Prufrock Press, 2008.
- Walker, Sally M. *Written in Bone: Buried Lives of Jamestown and Colonial Maryland.* Carolhoda Books, 2009.

Resources

Websites

- About the FBI: *fbi.gov/fun-games/kids/kids-about*
  This official Federal Bureau of Investigation website contains information on forensics and the history of the FBI, as well as puzzles and games.

- Crash Scene Investigation: *edheads.org/activities/crash_scene/index.shtml*
  Examine the evidence of a deadly car crash.

- Crime Museum: *crimemuseum.org/interactive-games*
  Interactive games, including polls, quizzes, and riddles, will challenge your knowledge of forensics and policing.

- CSI, The Experience: Web Adventures: *forensics.rice.edu*
  An educational site connected to the *CSI* traveling exhibit with online games and activities.

- CSI Science: Get the Prints! *stem-works.com/subjects/11-biometrics/activities/176*
  In this activity, you can practice lifting prints.

- CyberBee: *cyberbee.com/whodunnit/crimescene.html*
  Read a crime report and meet the suspects as you solve "The Case of the Barefoot Burglar."

- Edu Web: The Art of Crime Detection: *eduweb.com/portfolio/artofcrimedetection*
  Participate in an interactive animation in which you help solve crimes.

- Go Cognitive Change Blindness Game: *gocognitive.net/demo/change-blindness*
  Crime scene investigators need to identify witnesses, but sometimes they are not very observant. This challenge will test your skills.

- Interactive Investigator: *virtualmuseum.ca/sgc-cms/expositions-exhibitions/detective-investigator/en/game/index.php*
  You can become an investigator in this interactive story and game.

- PBS Forensics and Investigations: *pbs.org/wgbh/nova/archive/int_inve.html*
  Watch clips from the PBS show *Nova* on famous forensic cases.

- Science Mystery: *sciencemystery.com*
  Use your problem-solving skills to solve any of the nine mysteries on this site.

- SFU Museum of Archaeology and Ethnology: *sfu.museum/forensics/eng*
  An interactive forensic game complete with interviews of forensic specialists.
  Content may be disturbing.

- Wonderville: *wonderville.ca/asset/fascinating-forensics*
  Perform the experiment from this site to learn how investigators decide which pen a victim or criminal may have used at a crime scene.

Resources

Careers

- Association of Women in Forensic Science: *awifs.org*
  The U.S.-based organization provides opportunities for young people who are interested in pursuing a career in forensic science.

- Crime Scene Investigators Network: *crime-scene-investigator.net/becomeone.html*
  The site explains how you can begin a career in crime-scene investigation.

- Not Invented Here LifeWorks: *nihlifeworks.org/Interviews/Angi%2bM.html*
  Watch an interview of forensic anthropologist Angi M. Christine.

Forensic Exhibits

- National Library of Medicine - Visible Proofs Forensic Views of the Body: *nlm.nih.gov/visibleproofs*
  A comprehensive site with several online exhibitions, including "The Rise of Forensics and Technologies of Surveillance." Galleries feature cases, biographies, artifacts, and more.

- Crime Museum: *crimemuseum.org*
  A Washington, D.C., museum that has online projects, games, quizzes, and information related to crime.

- Smithsonian Institution: *anthropology.si.edu/writteninbone*
  Web pages created for the "Written in Bone" exhibit that the museum hosted from 2009 to 2013. There are activities, photos, and online activities based on the exhibit that you can access.

QR Code Glossary

- Page 7: galton.org
- Page 10: vimeo.com/66937393
- Page 16: smithsonianmag.com/arts-culture/murder-miniature-nutshell-studies-unexplained-death-180949943/?no-ist
- Page 18: www2.le.ac.uk/study/why-us/discoveries/the-invention-of-dna-fingerprinting
- Page 45: fws.gov/lab/students.php
- Page 45: fws.gov/lab/pdfs/Smithsonian.pdf
- Page 50: kidshealth.org/kid/closet/movies/SSmovie.html?tracking = K_RelatedArticle
- Page 53: bbc.co.uk/programmes/b03w03bb
- Page 60: ucl.ac.uk/archaeology/research/projects/astypalaia/completepot
- Page 68: www.le.ac.uk/richardiii/science.html
- Page 68: youtube.com/watch?v = ge3LSCctDgQ
- Page 75: podcast.montgomerycollege.edu/podcast.php?rcdid = 22

Index

Index